We really enjoy your use of imagery, descriptive language and insight.

—**Pat Swenson**, Editor Emeritus,
Avocet, A Journal of Nature Poems

Besides being wonderful poems they have an undercurrent, sometimes a flood-tide of sensuality, Eros and Thanatos, which gives the book a life above and beyond the beautiful words.

—**George Spencer**, Co-host of ABC No Rio

Green Rain
Poems by
Mary Orovan

POETS WEAR PRADA • Hoboken, New Jersey

Green Rain

First North American Publication 2008.

Copyright © 2008 Mary Orovan

All rights reserved. Except for use in any review or for educational purposes, the reproduction or utilization of this work in whole or in part in any form by electronic, mechanical or other means, now known or hereafter invented, including xerography, photocopying and recording, or in any informational or retrieval system, is forbidden without the written permission of the publisher. Poets Wear Prada, 533 Bloomfield Street, Second Floor, Hoboken, New Jersey 07030.

http://pwpbooks.blogspot.com/

Grateful acknowledgment is made to the following journals where some of these poems have previously appeared:

Avocet, A Journal of Nature Poems; *Amoskeag*; *Freshwater*; and *The Fourth River*.

ISBN 978-0-9817678-5-7

Printed in the U.S.A.

Front Cover Design: Roxanne Hoffman
Author's Photo: Snapshot in Central Park by Jacob Stern

To Harrykin

Contents

Timely / 1
Brash / 2
Lushberries / 3
Inside Love / 4
UNDO / 4
Jacqueline du Pré Plays / 5
Edge / 6
Supple / 7
Feathers / 8
Growing Up / 9
Ms. Magoo / 10
Pornography in the Park / 11
It catches us after all / 12
April / 13
The Autumn of My Discontent / 14
snow angels / 15
How to Feel No Pain / 16
White Grass / 18
Moving / 19
Green Rain / 20

Acknowledgements

*There is a tree, a London plane,
its beauty wraps me in dreams of living
in the almost forever of its reaching.*

—Mary Orovan

Timely

Let me buy some time, said
    the rich man,
*I now buy someone to smooth
    every minute of what
I have.* But time looms large,
    inexorably forward.
I can crush it, said the witch
    on her sonic broom.

*Not fast enough—I'll take you
    there,* said light,
*if you observe at my speed
    I can make time
stand still—that's what you folks
    call paradise.*

    But I want to zag to the past,
embellish memories, laser on the hill
    of daisies where we first lay;

    zig to tomorrow
a dimension changing everything.

    Heaven is now; breathe &
be—shining with photons, transparent
    as good air   joy
the pure silence of not even ticking.

Brash

We curl along the paths
of summer   float
on dandelion parachutes
in heating air
we are hi silly
as hollyhocks,
sunflower brash,

and we don't care,
we are almost bare
in our halter tops
looking for the wild lake
where we bob blue
    clouds doodle stories,
fantasies
wave as we loft
nipples hard
in the fresh
of water
any every pore
stands &
giggles *alive*
    in tiger lily days.

Lushberries

Colors peak as summer
comes
strawberry
leaves
tease with pink
lift them
to pluck
the wild scarlet.

Tufting on bushes
raspberries
scream red.
Lush juices rouge
our tongues
as two-handed
we gobble
melting rubies.

In the plush of August
colors burn to darker purples
blacker blues.
Seedy blackberry, dusty blueberry
blend into shadows of shorter
afternoons and we grab
our pleasures

because after the grapes
it's all over.

Inside Love

I want to disrobe
your brain and live
in the blue-gray matter
of your being,

my apple mind growing
with knowledge of
your Eden.

We are almost Siamese,
brushed at the belly,
I can look only to your
amber eyes.

UNDO

Yellow leaf falls upward to tree

Warblers fly in reverse
  (Canada blocks border)
April lasts all summer

I didn't take that walk
    I never met you
        I never met you

Jacqueline du Pré Plays

   Curve of cello
between her knees

Mahogany furniture   Rembrandt
pregnant chiaroscuro

August hung fruit   the juices

Vibrato in toe tip throating
to mushroom eyes   moss

Layering apart the petals
  of a tea rose

Brandy entering   lingering
  strokes for a feral cat

Edge

at the cusp

frail beginning
on twig
baby finger anxious green

egg's hairline crack
shattering to life
our crowning
smack to cry

drop of blood
pop of question
get of idea

how it feels
suicide leap   second after

or slow inch by inch easing in
   the gliding wet
body swim head going under
   to the heart

final petal fall
drying pistil burned by time
fragile vapor on mirror

Supple

Enduring the color orange,
extremity of seasons,
boys carving
    deep initials,
families of birds,
    staying green
        in Spring snow

The shirt of God
    baby blue
Her skirts
    six shades of soil

Look   Study supple responses
    to fate:
        lightning and ice
            tentacles of cities
Time for the truth of trees,
    history of patience
        persistence,
One branch brought
        to the ground—suddenly
    twists up again
Still finding the high breast
    of the sun
        the milky opening of light

Feathers

We stand in shuddering snow
to watch the owl fly out,
animals tearing to burrows,
last flesh of dusk,
early moon rising metal pale.

Now. Immensity of ashen
wings refolding
on fringes of lowest fir.
All eye and claw.
Death ravishing in feathers.

Growing Up

There is a circus of crocus
and it's so nice to see
North finally coo spring in petals
      velvet persimmon   ice cream

white   best one I like
      lavender and royal
regal and silly and brave
all at the same

two-colored tutu flying
from a winter trapeze

and they fold at dusk like animals
    fleeing narrow owl   freezing night
promise of big girl days

the becoming of everything

among feathering trees

Ms. Magoo

Observer of hustle, rubble,
absolutely in love with life,
I peer near sighted:

Never wear glasses
if you can navigate the hazy
beauty of indefiniteness.

No trash at picnics in the park.

The small trees of the city
have pleasant arms.

A purple striped zebra
prances on Third Avenue.

Pornography in the Park

Public mating,
    out in the open,

   Grey owl has cozied
with Red owl
   in hollow hole
of the old Pin oak,
    fluffing each other's cheeks,
waiting for the moon.

And Pale Male and Lola,
   our City hawks, atop the Carlyle Hotel,
       aerobatic display,
always Valentine's day.

Indigo go go
  puffed puffed pigeons
followingcirclingfollowing,
   woo.   Bill and... .

  Egregious acts
of ubiquitous birds
    oh, baby, all over the City.

     Edgy music in the Ramble
  wild timbres and rhythms
bird calls
               bird calls
  birds answering
        love on the fly everywhere.

It catches us after all

While we danced
    there was dying
and when we kissed such
    painful illness and breaks
        in body and spirit.

As we flicked a cowlick
    adjusted the crease   fussed
over words said or not—there was a loss
    of all words—there was the room
        with only the caretaker

and a slit of light.
    Best we are mostly unaware,
for in our ripening years, twirling and doing,
    reality would weight us so;
        and if we are hurt in a car,

shed from work, when we
    can just mouth *tomorrow*,
memory softens to the hum of "busy".
    Eating up life, we try to dodge
        the daily eking drudge of most;

creeping infirmities
    of age; lurking vagaries
of luck. Something catches us.
    And yet   and yet joy,
        languorous brush of fingertips,

our brain's numinous
    lovely leaping to places new,
the giddy senses of love   its spill
   into even suffering
      ubiquitous as air.

April

Yes.

We can't hide from solace.

Everywhere we are swaddled

In the palest green of new buds

And baby grass.

The Autumn of My Discontent

I don't like being on this
   side of time,
     seeing friends slide, weaken,
the most brilliant eaten by dementia.

I always think I will be one of the
exceptions, setting the treadmill to
climb,
doing mental triple summersaults,
    if I can just
       ignore
         the
           trembling.

I so admire the rose
    in December,
her cyclamen
   frozen to sick damask pink
  creamy edges ochre and curled.
     Still exquisite,
      till white
        blankets
         her
          bravado.

snow angels

flapped by tots they dot the hillocks of Central Park on any mound a $500 sled or pieces of cardboard kids playing miniature luge on thin latte of snow sugaring faces and paws of dogs some in *Casa Bow Wow* coats children in a Fifth Avenue hat parade peaks & balls bobbing colorcombocollage everyone scraping a cool only snow day of winter

remembering Uncle Marcel's toboggan 7-seater we'd tummy on like layers of strudel atop atop in asexual delight at G-force toward traffic of Montreal's Park Ave neverfailedtostop even when we decided to do it upside down and backwards our eyes praying skyward no fence against daring months & months of snow to practice specially standing up (before snow boards) we were pioneers little devils and angels of the slope

How to Feel No Pain
The truth is a matter of the imagination.
—Ursala K. Le Guin, *The Left Hand of Darkness*

Urania knows which planet to pick
she has traveled to them all
as I pace this nervous, pallid chamber
I envision Inverse Hypochondria

Where *doctors* molder
in waiting rooms
with only yellow furniture
crumpled magazines
nurses calling first names

Finally left in tissue gowns
on icy tables
forever

While
We live inside flowers
eating honey, sleeping on satin

It rains only on Tuesday, enough
to keep the planet purple, our color of choice
sometimes We work on beautifying projects
creating pointed shoes
for the rare times We walk on the ground
our wings folded in origami
in all eleven dimensions

We play word games
but equations solve themselves

Merely breathing We compose music
forgotten notes echo, echo
in choruses that can be heard
on most of our 23 moons

We are the right hand of lightness
hermaphrodites
flying attached in circles and swirls
like fireflies

White Grass

My chin sprouts stubble—
   white grass—I am becoming my
environment—a slip of a thing
   from whom people look away—
no breasts heaving promise—
   almost part of trees, yet unsturdy,
unsteady; shuffle of awful steps,

   dry ground before wind.
Though rain will not resurrect or caress
   new budding—I still think how
I might ask God to be honey.
   Dark chocolate melts sweetless
in an old mouth if you are alone.

Moving

Yeasty waves make lacy loops
leaving toe prints
washing them away
smoothing the shifting sand
nothing is still

Cycle of up and down
the supreme pleasure of it
apogee   perigee   spring and fall
planet tilts   a world twirling
undulating stars
light in pellets and waves

Not even ice is static
hardening   then sliding into
fecundity

To not move is to die

But decay is movement too
another time
in something else's need
peristalsis and orifices everywhere

And all of the wonder is
in the moving
the sturdy beating
then galloping
of the heart
at your approach

Green Rain

Apricot Trumpet Vines
    rose to life
opening long throats
    to water

Curling wither of grass,
    September's umber,
almost again the porcelain
    lime of youth

True, there are orange
    Rose Hips hard among buds,
but the wilding Pinks,
    beloved of bees,
receive multiple visits

Dahlias, fuchsia meringue,
    sit atop
slicked mint purple stems,
    on their leaves,
bubbles rainbow in the sun

Soon Mallard heads turn
    emerald again,
a second green coming

  And in the Milkweed
    the chrysalis of tomorrow

Acknowledgements

"Brash" *Avocet, A Journal of Nature Poems*, Summer 2008

"Lushberries" *Avocet, A Journal of Nature Poems*, Summer 2008

"UNDO" *Amoskeag,* Spring 2008

"Supple" *Freshwater,* Spring 2008

"The Autumn of My Discontent" *The Fourth River,* Fall 2006

"Green Rain" *Avocet, A Journal of Nature Poems,* Fall 2007

Special thanks to Elaine Reiman and George Spencer for their wise suggestions.

Thank you, too, to the other members of Jefferson Market Library Poetry Workshop in Greenwich Village, NYC, where many of these poems were first read.

www.ingramcontent.com/pod-product-compliance
Lightning Source LLC
Chambersburg PA
CBHW061519040426
42450CB00008B/1690